Poetry of
BEN VERONA

Blue Goose Books LLC,
P.O. Box 1430, Linden, NJ 07036
bluegoosebooks@gmail.com

Copyright © Blue Goose Books 2017
All rights reserved. This book may not be reproduced or transmitted in any form, or by any electronic, mechanical, or other means, without written permission from the publisher, except by a reviewer, who may include brief quotations in a review. Written permission to reproduce or transmit any part of this book may be requested from the publisher at bluegoosebooks@gmail.com or at Blue Goose Books, P.O. Box 1430, Linden, NJ 07036.

Library of Congress Control Number: 2015940112

International Standard Book Numbers (ISBN)
Softcover Paperback: 978-0-9833629-1-3
eBook: 978-0-9833629-2-0
Audio Book: 978-0-9833629-3-7

PUBLISHER'S INTRODUCTION

Our objective at Blue Goose Books is to publish works that inform, enlighten, and entertain. When a work achieves one or more of these goals, we are pleased to publish it. When we are able to publish a work that achieves all three of these goals, we feel privileged to have made a social and cultural contribution of lasting value.

Ben Verona is a new voice in poetry. His poetry speaks simply, directly, passionately, and sometimes humorously, about the human condition. This is poetry rooted in those fertile fields of human experience common to us all. **LIFELINES** takes a fresh and unique look at important aspects of our human condition, aspects we often lose sight of as we live in the busy circumstances of our daily lives. Much of this poetry brings us back to lost or forgotten thoughts, feelings, and experiences, refocuses them, and opens for us the door of renewed human possibilities. This poetry is a body of work with unique insight and focus, that we are privileged to publish.

Part of our editorial process involves arranging poems thematically for our readers. For us, these poems fall into five broad thematic categories, and we have arranged them thematically within these categories. These are:

- *Human Condition–Human Possibilities*
- *Open or Closed*
- *Love and Relationships*
- *Transcendent Experience*
- *Wild Imaginings*

The poems in **Wild Imaginings** take a fanciful look at our relationships with some of the wild things in nature with whom we share this planet.

Transcendent Experience is a category of poems that explore some of those unique life experiences capable of transporting us into that special realm of reality and experience that transcends the circumstances of our daily lives. These poems provide us with a unique look at our ability to have such transcendent experiences and open for us the possibility of enriching our lives with them.

Love and Relationships contains poems that address and explore what love is, what it means, and what it takes for us to get there. Some of this poetry explores love that loses sight of itself and causes us to treat ourselves, and our beloveds badly, and not from love at all.

The poems in *Open or Closed* suggest that we are capable of being closed to anything, even love. They also explore the personal consequences of such closures, and refocus for us the innate ability we all have to open ourselves to love, and all of the other wonders of human experience available to us.

Poetry in the category *Human Condition-Human Possibilities* explores aspects of our human condition in the context of our experiences in the world and the events that occur around us, and that affect us physically and emotionally. In that exploration, this poetry opens for us unique portals of positive human possibility, and leaves to us the ongoing personal exploration of those possibilities.

Across all categories, the poetry in **LIFELINES** is engaging, enlightening, thought-provoking, and entertaining. Its imagery is clear and powerful, and its humorous aspects, often subtle, are always playful, fanciful, and delightful.

We hope you enjoy this poetry as much as we have, and submit it to all of our readers to enjoy and experience for themselves. We appreciate and respect the highly personal and subjective nature of the experience that each individual reader has with books. We understand and appreciate that reading is an essentially interactive experience, and that each reader participates uniquely and individually in that experience. So, we present **LIFELINES** to our readers with that understanding, and invite their comments via e-mail at *bluegoosebooks@gmail.com*, or by mail to Blue Goose Books, P.O. Box 1430, Linden, NJ 07036.

FORMAT: We want our books to be not only informative, enlightening and entertaining – but reader friendly, and useful. To that end, we have indexed this poetry by titles, and with opening lines; and we have included some blank note pages at the back of the book for the personal use of our readers.

TABLE OF CONTENTS

Publisher's Introduction 1
Index of Titles–Sequential with Opening Lines 7
Category Headings
      Human Condition–Human Possibilities 11
      Open or Closed 41
      Love and Relationships 49
      Transcendent Experience 61
      Wild Imaginings 69
Note Pages 74
Index of Titles - Alphabetical with Opening Lines 79

INDEX OF TITLES
SEQUENTIAL WITH OPENING LINES

*** HUMAN CONDITION-HUMAN POSSIBILITIES ***

THE T.V. GEE VEES 13
I must have the T.V. gee vees

ACTORS AND AUTHORS 14
Actors live to be seen and not heard

THE BRAVEST THING OF ALL 15
To lose all fear

MONEY, LOVE AND JIVE 16
So afraid of dying, so happy to just be alive

GIVE AND TAKE 17
When to press and when to yield

FROM THE COUPLING 18
We are from the coupling of God and nature

THE TRUTH 20
The dead are truly happy

WASHINGTON MONUMENT 21
Old George was a funky dude

BITTER END 22
Don't live life like all there is

COMMITMENT 23
Total commitment no matter what

TWISTED 24
Twisted, turned, shaped, formed

GOOD GUYS AND BAD GUYS 25
Violence is ambivalent. It floats

9-1-1 26
    On 9 - 1 - 1 – the TV said

THE WELL 27
    At the bottom of the well of self-worth

THE WORLD 28
    The world is full of danger

THE FIX 29
    The fix is in

SADDER SCENE 30
    Has there ever been a sadder scene

CHILDREN CAN SUCCEED 31
    Children can succeed where parents fail

UNGRATEFUL 32
    I suppose they thought or felt

BETTER THAN A DREAM 33
    Born to a clamor of cultures

NEVER DONE 34
    What always seemed so far away, is ever so close at hand

THE BUSINESS OF DYING 35
    In the business of dying salvation gets sold

THE IMPORTANCE OF NOT KNOWING 36
    The Golden Key
    To The Gilded Lock
    On The Ancient Oak and Iron Door

STORIES 37
    How important to have a story

THESE EYES 38
    These eyes through which I see the world

FEELINGS 39
   Feelings come and go.

*** OPEN OR CLOSED ***

NEVER TOLD 43
   Like a door that we can open, but for safety we keep closed

THE HEART HAS TWO KEYS 44
   The heart has two keys

TURTLES 45
   Turtles are a lot like people

SOMEDAY 46
   Beauty, grace and power flow from loin to limb

FOREVER ONE 47
   I embrace you, and open myself to you

LUCKY IN LIFE 48
   If you are lucky in life

*** LOVE AND RELATIONSHIPS ***

LOVE IS 51
   Love is a choice
   We make
      Or not

LOVE NEEDS 52
   Romantic love needs reassurance

WHAT MEN NEED MOST 53
   What men need most from the women they love

ONCE AGAIN 54
   "It's gone too long," she said

BEHOLD 55
   When you take me into the dark abyss

VERY OFTEN ABSENT 56
   Very often absent, even when you're here

WANTED AS A LOVER 57
   Wanted as a lover, never as a friend

THAT GOLDEN DREAM 58
   Not far off, I saw a shining - shimmering five point perfect star

* * * TRANSCENDENT EXPERIENCE * * *

NIAGARA 63
   Niagara – amazing in its beauty,
   metaphoric in its magic, transcendent in its glory

THE PARADOX OF YOU 65
   You, the superficial one

ENLIGHTENED DESCARTES 66
   I think – therefore I am?

UNSPOKEN 67
   A kiss, caress, a tender touch

THE PALACE OF CIALIS 68
   Over time and with age

* * * WILD IMAGININGS * * *

ONE OF THE ANIMALS 71
   One of the animals who lives in the sea

ROUND ABOUT 72
   Are we so different now

NATURAL LAW 73
   When in the grass

HUMAN CONDITION
– HUMAN POSSIBILITIES

THE T.V. GEE VEES

I must have the T. V. Gee Vees,
My body craves what it provides,

That beam of light and conversation,
Hits me right between the eyes,

That special brand of relaxation,
Oh God! I need it to survive,

I must have the T. V. Gee Vees,
To be connected - is to be alive.

ACTORS AND AUTHORS

Actors live to be seen
And not heard.
They give presence and place
To the words of authors.

Authors live to be heard
And not seen,
Except through characters
Brought to life by actors.

Actors and authors together
Create the stories,
The images,
The myths,
And beliefs,

From which
We take meaning,
And in which
We live our lives.

Actors and authors together-
What would life be
Without them?

THE BRAVEST THING OF ALL

To lose all fear
I once thought
The bravest thing of all

But then recalled
I'd had that thought
Many times before

So time's now come
To recognize
Fear's programmed
For recall

There's nothing wrong
With having fear
It's there always
In us all

With all of this
I now know
The bravest things become
Not I think
To lose all fear
But what is to be done

Now what's to do
Is up to me
When fear is on recall

And now I know
That just to choose
Is the bravest thing of all

MONEY, LOVE AND JIVE

So afraid of dying,
So happy to just be alive,
Nothing else seems to matter,
Not money, love or jive

To lose that fear of flying,
Is to live not just survive,
With all life's joys and pleasures,
Money, love
and jive

GIVE AND TAKE

When to press
And when to yield,
When to thrust
And when to shield,

Are decisions
We all must make,
To play life's game
Of Give and Take.

But when our sense
Of others dies,
Or blind anger
Fills our eyes,

When to press
And when to yield,
When to thrust
And when to shield,

Are decisions
We do not make,
And lose
Life's game
Of Give and Take.

FROM THE COUPLING

We are from the coupling
Of God and Nature.

You say you doubt that coupling!

Why else " God the Father "?

Why else "Mother Nature"?

Without that coupling,
Would nature
Suckle us,
Nourish us,
Provide for us,
And sustain us?

Would God
Be Father to us,
Guide us,
Enlighten us,
And protect us?

As the children
Of God and Nature
We are blest with parents
Who provide for us
Body and soul

We are born from them intact,
With spirit, flesh, and seeds
So that as we ripen
And become ready
Our seeds are planted
And grow again-

All in a way
As magical as the morning
And as fresh
As the spirit of that coupling.

THE TRUTH

The dead are truly happy.

In that final pristine moment,
On the bridge
Between life and death,

They have seen both shores clearly,
Known the truth,

And forgiven everything.

WASHINGTON MONUMENT

Old George
was a funky dude,

Whose claims to fame
did include,

An organ that was
very huge.

So in his name
we did erect

A monument
to that effect,

For all the world
to know and see,

What really matters
To you and me.

BITTER END

Don't live life
Like all there is
So much so
When life's all gone
There will be left
A bitter taste - a bitter end.

What most we do
To void that loss
is live our lives
As not so much to lose

And in that way
Lose all the best
Before it's gone

Just to end up right!

COMMITMENT

Total commitment no matter what

Can come to life like a crystal spring
Bubbly and clear

Or like a conversation in the marketplace
That seeks and bargains for itself,
Finds the price too dear,
And then withdraws.

TWISTED

Twisted, turned,
Shaped, formed,
Popped-out molded,
Never born,

Sometimes glimpsed,
Seldom seen,
Spotlight search,
Hot white beam,

Twisted, turned,
Shaped, formed,
Grown, cultured,
Ripped and torn,
Popped-out molded,

But never born.

GOOD GUYS AND BAD GUYS

Violence is ambivalent. It floats.

The law's against it,
Except -
It's o.k. to kill
Bad guys.

But bad guys are
Good guys
To somebody.

And good guys
Are bad guys
To somebody.

So it's okay - to kill everybody?

Violence is ambivalent. It floats.

9-1-1

(Nine - One - One)

On 9-1-1 the TV said:

*Thousands and thousands
are probably dead.*

On 9-1-1 the politicians said:

*Let us join together as Americans
and in that way honor our dead.*

On 9-1-1 the graffiti said:

*Lets kill those bastards
to avenge the dead.*

But on 9-1-1 the sidewalk said:

*An eye for an eye
leaves everybody dead.*

THE WELL

At the bottom of the well of self worth,
When empty, when dry,

We cling to the stones
On the walls,
To the empty bucket,
The slack rope,
And the dry earth,

As though our lives
Depend on them,

Instead of looking for water elsewhere,
And risk finding nothing.

THE WORLD

The world is full of danger,
And we must go boldly to it,
Confront it, explore it,
Dominate, and tame it.

Otherwise, we will never be safe.

THE FIX

The fix is in,
everything's set,
beginning, middle and end.

So take your best shots,
make your best bets,
and prolong
for as long as you can-

Cause the fix is in
and it'll take time
for you to play out your hand.

SADDER SCENE

Has there ever been
A sadder scene,

Than a person
Who's given up
On a dream.

Just maybe
Even sadder still

Is that dreamer's life
Lived unfulfilled.

CHILDREN CAN SUCCEED

Children can succeed
Where parents fail

When they are open
To what to do,

To make life better
Than what they knew.

UNGRATEFUL

I suppose they thought or felt
That gratitude would grow in us
If the seeds were planted early
And at every opportunity.

I suppose they thought
Those seeds would grow in us
If we saw ourselves as burdens,
And the source of pains in necks and asses.

I often wonder now
If they see beyond
The cutting edge
Of our kitchen table confrontations.

I suppose they see us as ungrateful.

BETTER THAN A DREAM

Born to a clamor of cultures,
Subcultures, cities, states,
Cars, buses, planes and trains,

A fullness of families,
Aunts, uncles, cousins, friends,
Parents, grandparents, brothers, sisters,
Neighbors, and neighborhoods,

Schools, playgrounds,
Buildings, stairs, stoops and sidewalks,
Streets and alleyways,
Alive and bristling
With danger and the dark presence of death,

And slicing through it all,
The great transcendent beam of television,
That beautiful beam of light, of language, of hope,
A world of people progress, opportunity, success and acceptance,

Somewhere to go to, a worth getting to place,
Away from the personal insults
Of not enough of everything you want,
And too much of everything you don't.

The people and the language
That came through that screen,
Were more than real,
Were better than a dream.

NEVER DONE

What always seemed so far away,
Is ever so close at hand,

That paradox of time and space,
I do not understand.

What paradox of space, of time,
Not cause effected like the rising sun,

Brings acceptance, then gives way,
To the living of life as never done.

THE BUSINESS OF DYING

In the business of dying
Salvation gets sold,
Payment's expected
And always in gold.

Belief and devotion
Are part of that deal,
Part of the bargain,
Its sense and its feel.

But truth of the matter,
When the story gets told,
Salvation for living
Is worth more than gold.

So buyer be cautious,
And buyer beware,
In the business of dying
The bargain's not fair.

THE IMPORTANCE OF NOT KNOWING

The Golden Key
To The Gilded Lock
On The Ancient Oak and Iron Door

That Opens
To The Pathway Of The Spirit

Is Not Knowledge

But The Awareness And Acceptance
Of The Importance Of Not Knowing

STORIES

How important
To have a story,

To believe it
And live in it,

To wear it well
Like a custom tailored suit
To show the world,

Until it wears beyond repair,
Or the fashion changes.

THESE EYES

These eyes through which I see the world

Do not tell me who I am, or how to be
But bring to me a world alive
To be in and to see

And all the rest of how that is
Is up to me, is up to me.

FEELINGS

Feelings come and go.
I am constant.

Feelings ebb and flow.
I am not my feelings.

If my feelings bid me follow,
must I, like slave to master go?

Or say instead – "Thank you but no."

Then chart my own course,
And look to see,

If those feelings then,
Will follow me.

OPEN OR CLOSED

NEVER TOLD

Like a door
That we can open
But for safety
We keep closed

Like a window
In the winter
That we shut
Against the cold

Like the shutters
On our windows
That we close
Against the storm

Our hearts
That can be broken
We close
To keep from harm.

And when the love
We all have need of
Is kept out
Just like the cold

In the safety
Of our shelters
We soon
Grow very old

And the life
Behind our windows
Becomes a story
Never told.

THE HEART HAS TWO KEYS

The heart
Has two keys,

Like a safe deposit box
That cannot be opened
Without them.

I have one.

Do you have the other?

TURTLES

Turtles are a lot like people.
They carry their armor with them,
Expose little of themselves,
And are always ready to draw back in.

But mighty Hermaphrodity has not visited turtles,
And so to survive, they come together
And shed their shells
In exploding oceans of sexual ecstasy.

In those moments,
They expose themselves,
And risk everything,
For each other, and for life.

Unshelled, they float freely,
In the warm soft water,
And enjoy the sun.

But such times for turtles,
Are few and far between,
For danger lurks everywhere,
And calls them back in.

And so they return,
To the safety of their shells,
To plod along,
Until the next outcoming.

SOMEDAY

Beauty, Grace and Power
Flow from loin to limb,

A house of pure desire
Burning from within,

But missing always missing
Is that total self release,

That feeling of surrender
That place of total peace.

FOREVER ONE

I embrace you,
And open myself
to you,

And invite you
To open yourself
To me,

So that we may flow
Into each other

And become one,
In the moment
And forever.

LUCKY IN LIFE

If you are lucky in life
A good woman
Will choose you,

And make this known to you
In wondrous ways.

She will take you
Into her heart
And into her life.

She will give herself
To you as a gift,
And make you feel wanted,
Make you feel needed,
And make you feel loved.

So be wise,
And be open
To such luck,
So you can recognize
And welcome it
When it comes.

You will always
Be thankful
That you did.

LOVE AND RELATIONSHIPS

LOVE IS

Love is a choice
We make
        Or not.

Love is a risk
We take
        Or not.

Then Love is heartfelt,

        Or not,
Really Love at all.

LOVE NEEDS

Romantic love
needs reassurance
of love returned,

And so seeks
words and acts
of love
to satisfy that need,

And avoid the dread
of love lost,

Or worse,

Of having been wrong
From the beginning,

And a fool
About it all.

WHAT MEN NEED MOST

What men need most
From the women they love,
Is to know that they have made them happy.

Without that,
Men feel no joy,
And withdraw from the pain of knowing

That they have failed
In the most important work
They will ever do.

ONCE AGAIN

"It's gone too long," she said.

"How long," I asked.
"Too long to remember,"
"Too long to still feel."

"It's gone too far," she said.

"How far," I asked.
"Too far to get back,"
"Too far to still touch."

Listen, please listen,
Old friend, old friend.

What we once had,
We can have once again,
But only if we say so,
And when we say when.

BEHOLD

When you take me
Into the dark abyss
Of the Taken for Granted
And the Easily Forgotten,

In your eyes,
The eyes of the beholder,
Behold your own truth,

And know
It is not mine.

VERY OFTEN ABSENT

Very often absent
Even when you're here

Brings a rush of sadness
Brings a silent tear

Brings back buried feelings
Of rejection, doubt and fear

Very often absent
Even when you're here.

WANTED AS A LOVER

Wanted as a lover
Never as a friend

Object of desire
For lust that knew no end

Failed to see love missing
In that mixture
And that blend

Wanted as a lover
Never as a friend

THAT GOLDEN DREAM

Not far off, I saw a shining-shimmering
five point perfect star,
dancing with reflected light,
just above the glistening water
of that summer night's sea.

As I watched,
I felt drawn to that star
by some basic elemental need
only that star could fill.

There was no wind, so I could not sail,
and I was afraid to break apart
with cranky engine noise
that fragile midnight mix
of summer sea and light.

The dinghy then would be my transport
for a closer look at that dazzling, dancing star.

As I rowed, the only sounds that ran
and echoed inside that night's silent shell
came from the oars as they together softly splushed
into and out of the glistening water.

I rowed for what seemed like hours,
until my aching arms and body
screamed that I should row no more.

But then I felt the warm moist glow
of that star's light reflect soft against my skin,
and saw and knew at once,
that it was almost close enough to touch.

The prospect of touching that golden dream
and of having it for my own
fell upon me like some primal scream,
and I rowed with new and frantic force.

But the distance now would not close,
the harder I rowed the further away
we seemed to be,
until at last my twice exhausted self
could row no more.

As I sat transfixed,
so near yet so far away,
a gently breeze began to blow
and push away that dazzling star
until its light faded and then
disappeared.

I raised a clenched defiant fist and shouted–"Shit!"

Then sharply dipped the starboard oar
to turn and row away

And said or thought
to sooth my savaged soul-

"So what!"
"She was probably a lousy cook,
and worse in bed anyway."

TRANSCENDENT EXPERIENCE

TRANSCENDENTALISM

NIAGARA

Niagara-
Amazing in its beauty,
Metaphoric in its magic,
Transcendent in its glory!

Above the falls,
The river,
Wide and dark,
Bristling brown and green,
Flows full and steady
Ever onward
With powerful primal force.

At the falls,
At the edge of the abyss,
The river's waters
Turn crystal white
And translucent green

Then pure crystal white,
Blue and black
As they fall
From that lofty precipice
Down the sheer rock face
To the rocky shores below.

In the roaring crash,
The fallen river
Transforms
Into white, translucent mist

That rises and transcends
The rocky edge
From which it plunged.

The rising mist forms
Pure white puffs
That join and rejoin
Into billowing fluffy,
Sun tinged clouds,

Which in time
Will release the river's water
As drops of rain
To fall and rejoin their kind
In the surging river below.

And so repeats
The endless cycle
Of transformation and renewal
That is Niagara—

Most sacred, most spiritual of all waters,

Amazing in its beauty,
Metaphoric in its magic,
Transcendent in its glory!

THE PARADOX OF YOU

You,
The superficial one,
The mask,
The act,
The programmed you,
The self protective you,
The defensive you.

To live life fully,
That you
Must find a way
To open to the true you,
The real, the unprotected,
The loving, vulnerable, caring you,

The one you cannot know
Or understand,
But can experience
In a way
That transcends everything.

That you, that self,
Is there always,
Worldly and divine,
At the center of creation.

ENLIGHTENED DESCARTES

I think - therefore I am?
If I don't think, do I cease to exist?

I think not!

And fall instead
Into the thought free land
Of experience,

Where in the pure joy
Of thoughtless presence,
I experience myself,

And know that I am.

UNSPOKEN

A kiss, caress, a tender touch,
Hello, a welcome, unspoken, felt,

A hand, run down the arched and settled slopes
of shoulders, back and buttocks,

Like some far off lilac and lavender misted mountains,
where dew moistens morning leaves,
and the smell of rain rises from the forest floor.

Time gone, self gone, all gone.

Sunlight shot through silver clouds
opens a ring of bright water
on an emerald bay,

Tides and currents
ebb and flow,

And waves wash gently
on the endless shore.

THE PALACE OF CIALIS

Over time
And with age
Some men come to dwell
In the palace of Cialis,

Where with the vigor of Viagra
They join again in that coupling
That transports them
To where love lives,

And to where
They can safely surrender themselves
To their lovers, and to love -

All in the magical mating mix
Of love and sex,
That in the moment,
Transcends everything.

And in the quiet after,
As they love,
And feel loved,
And cared about-
They are grateful,
And give thanks.

Thank you God!
Thank you Science!
Thank you all-
Who have helped create
And prolong this pleasure!
Thank you! Thank you! Thank you!

WILD IMAGININGS

ONE OF THE ANIMALS

One of the animals
Who lives in the sea,
Is bigger and wider
And rounder than me.

He is warm,
He is soft,
He thinks and
He breathes,

As he swims through the waves
With the greatest of ease,
Lives with his mate,
And spouts in the breeze.

Sometimes I do think him
An ancestor indeed.

ROUND ABOUT

Are we really now
Different than
The egg-eating blue jay,
The fish-eating otter playing in the open sea,
The round-bellied grass-grazing zebra,
The antelope-stalking lion?

King of beasts!

King of the jungle!

We eat everything!

NATURAL LAW

When in the grass
And bitten by insects
Too small to see,

And I learn of this
By the itch
From the bites
They take of me,

I am struck
By the injustice
Of being eaten
By things I cannot see,

And wonder how
Such injustice
Could have ever
Come to be.

NOTES

NOTES

NOTES

NOTES

NOTES

INDEX OF TITLES
ALPHABETICAL with OPENING LINES

ACTORS AND AUTHORS 14
    Actors live to be seen and not heard

BEHOLD 55
    When you take me into the dark abyss

BETTER THAN A DREAM 33
    Born to a clamor of cultures

BITTER END 22
    Don't live life like all there is

CHILDREN CAN SUCCEED 31
    Children can succeed where parents fail

COMMITMENT 23
    Total commitment no matter what

ENLIGHTENED DESCARTES 66
    I think – therefore I am?

FEELINGS 39
    Feelings come and go.

FOREVER ONE 47
    I embrace you, and open myself to you

FROM THE COUPLING 18
    We are from the coupling of God and nature

GIVE AND TAKE 17
    When to press and when to yield

GOOD GUYS AND BAD GUYS 25
    Violence is ambivalent. It floats

LOVE IS 51
    Love is a choice
    We make
        Or not

LOVE NEEDS 52
    Romantic love needs reassurance

LUCKY IN LIFE 48
    If you are lucky in life

MONEY, LOVE AND JIVE 16
    So afraid of dying, so happy to just be alive

NATURAL LAW 73
    When in the grass

NEVER DONE 34
    What always seemed so far away, is ever so close at hand

NEVER TOLD 43
    Like a door that we can open, but for safety we keep closed

NIAGARA 63
    Niagara – amazing in its beauty,
    metaphoric in its magic, transcendent in its glory

9-1-1 26
    On 9 - 1 - 1 – the TV said

ONCE AGAIN 54
    "It's gone too long," she said

ONE OF THE ANIMALS 71
    One of the animals who lives in the sea

ROUND ABOUT 72
    Are we so different now

SADDER SCENE 30
   Has there ever been a sadder scene

SOMEDAY 46
   Beauty, grace and power flow from loin to limb

STORIES 37
   How important to have a story

THAT GOLDEN DREAM 58
   Not far off, I saw a shining - shimmering five point perfect star

THE BRAVEST THING OF ALL 15
   To lose all fear

THE BUSINESS OF DYING 35
   In the business of dying salvation gets sold

THE HEART HAS TWO KEYS 44
   The heart has two keys

THE FIX 29
   The fix is in

THE IMPORTANCE OF NOT KNOWING 36
   The Golden Key
   To The Gilded Lock
   On The Ancient Oak and Iron Door

THE PALACE OF CIALIS 68
   Over time and with age

THE PARADOX OF YOU 65
   You, the superficial one

THE TRUTH 20
   The dead are truly happy

THE T.V. GEE VEES 13
   I must have the T.V. gee vees

THE WELL 27
    At the bottom of the well of self-worth

THE WORLD 28
    The world is full of danger

THESE EYES 38
    These eyes through which I see the world

TURTLES 45
    Turtles are a lot like people

TWISTED 24
    Twisted, turned, shaped, formed

UNGRATEFUL 32
    I suppose they thought or felt

UNSPOKEN 67
    A kiss, caress, a tender touch

VERY OFTEN ABSENT 56
    Very often absent, even when you're here

WANTED AS A LOVER 57
    Wanted as a lover, never as a friend

WASHINGTON MONUMENT 21
    Old George was a funky dude

WHAT MEN NEED MOST 53
    What men need most from the women they love

www.ingramcontent.com/pod-product-compliance
Lightning Source LLC
Chambersburg PA
CBHW071737040426
42446CB00012B/2383